Indoor Salad Gardening

Andrew Perkins

ISBN:1482567008
ISBN-13:9781482567007

DEDICATION

To my dear wife, who hears the car door slam, then an hour later comes out to see me digging in the garden – with my good shoes on, or finds me in the cellar, with my tie in the potting mix.

CONTENTS

INTRODUCTION

Living in US Zone 5 and 1200 feet above sea level, our growing season is shorter than those only two miles away and six hundred feet lower. With only three and one-half months of typical growing (we don't plant much before the end of May), we do what we can to extend the growing season. It's great to have fresh veggies when there is two feet of snow on the garden without having to put on boots! In this book you will discover:

Why You Should Grow an Indoor Salad Garden

What You Can You Grow in an Indoor Salad Garden

Where You Can Grow an Indoor Salad Garden

How Close to Place Your Grow Lights

When You Can You Grow an Indoor Salad Garden

How much room you will need vs how many salads you can expect

Specific Container Sizes and Needs for Popular Plants

Typical Indoor Garden Maladies and Remedies

1. WHY GROW AN INDOOR SALAD GARDEN?

An indoor garden allows you to grow your own vegetable year-round, no matter what the weather! You have control of the temperature, the humidity, the amount and type of light your plants get and what type of nutrition they (and ultimately you) get! Having a garden indoors also protects the plants from most critters that would eat them before you do, too.

People have been growing gardens indoors for centuries. Back in the Roman Empire, they used to grow cucumber-like plants in carts, wheeling them into the sun during the day, and bringing them inside at night (http://en.wikipedia.org/wiki/Greenhouse#History). Greenhouses in the U.S. that are still standing from the 19th century include the Lyman House in Waltham, MA, the Linnean House, built in 1882, at the Missouri Botanical Garden in St. Louis, and one in Guthrie OK, created by a man named Furrow.

Having food that is organically grown and fresh are two of the main reasons to grow an indoor salad garden. You know what has gone into growing it, what has and has not been sprayed on it, and your food source is always nearby. Apartment dwellers have the benefit of having fresh food any day of the year without having to travel. Fresh salads and vegetables also make great gifts - imaging receiving (or giving) a basket of fresh lettuce, cucumbers, chives and tomatoes during the winter holidays, or when cabin fever has reached its limit.

When spring finally arrives, if you have timed things right, you can have a jump on your outdoor garden! After hardening off, your plants will be further along than seeds you have planted, and allows you to have a longer harvest.

Summer heat does not bode well for lettuce unless you get the proper varieties or you are collecting seeds. The heat makes lettuce "bolt" - or go to seed which creates bitter greens, unsuitable for eating. Growing lettuce indoors allows them to stay cool where you can pick the outer leaves as you need them.

"*Who loves a garden loves a greenhouse too."*

William Cowper

1731-1800

2. WHAT CAN YOU GROW IN AN INDOOR SALAD GARDEN?

Photo Credit left: striatic http://www.flickr.com/photos/striatic/772121262/
Used under the Creative Commons Attribution License as of 2013/02/14

Photo Credit Center: http://www.flickr.com/photos/ejchang/4024771852/
Used under the creative Commons and Attributions and Share Alike License as of 2013/02/22

Photo Credit right: Kasia!! http://www.flickr.com/photos/failty/2604198420/
Used under the Creative Commons Attribution License as of 2012/02/22

You can grow many types of vegetables indoors. Lettuce does extremely well as long as the potting mix and temperature stays cool. Tomatoes and cucumbers prefer warm soil and air. Here is a list of some of the salad garden vegetables you can grow:

- Lettuce -
    - **loose leaf varieties**, such as "Vulcan"
    - salad mix "greens" - picked young and frequently – often planted together. Mixes often include Green Oakleaf, Red Oakleaf, Green Romaine, Red Romaine, deer tongue, Teide Summer Crisp, Black Seeded Simpson
    - **Mini Head Lettuces** such as Bambi Bibb Lettuce, Barbados, Focea Bibb Lettuce, Claremont, Lollo Rosa, Tom Thumb. Garden Babies and more.
- Chives (onions)
- Radishes
- Spinaches
- "Micro Greens"
- "Mini Greens: beet tops, broccoli rabe, kale, arugula, etc.
- Endives
- Herbs, such as Basil, Parsley, Cilantro
- Snow Peas (dwarf)
- Peas (dwarf, such as Tom Thumb)

Warmer Temperature Plants

- Tomatoes
- Peppers
- Green Beans
- Carrots (fingerlings)
- Strawberries
- Cucumbers

While there are "hard-core" indoor gardeners that will successfully grow corn in their living room (see http://www.wikihow.com/Grow-Corn-Indoors), most people will opt for plants they can grow indoors with much less effort. Do experiment! Once you have grown some salads, try other plant varieties too. There are dwarf & container varieties of many types of plants, including melons, brassicas, & more. Each will present their own challenges & needs, & if you grow a cantaloupe in the middle of your living room, you'll be the talk of the town!

3. WHERE CAN I GROW MY INDOOR SALAD GARDEN?

Photo Credit: tillwe - http://www.flickr.com/photos/tillwe/3341506183/
Used under the Creative Commons Attribution License as of 2013/02/14

There are eight considerations for your indoor garden that will determine what you can grow, and how much. These are:

a. **Space**
b. **Light**
c. **Heat**
d. **Humidity**
e. **Water**
f. **Growth Medium**
g. **Containers**
h. **Fertilizer**

(a) Space will be your first consideration. Many people don't have much unused space, but with a little creative rearranging you can create a "green nook" someplace in your home. If you have two feet by three feet of space (6 square feet), you can grow up to one salad per night if you pick the leaves from the plants instead of waiting until the plants are at full maturity and harvest the whole plant. Many people will plant the whole area lightly, and eat the thinnings. Setting up two of these (on a shelf or a small table) will of course yield twice as much, and give you some variety for lower growing plants. If you are intending to grow larger plants such as tomatoes or vining plants, you will need to keep this area as one six square foot area and have the ability to raise and lower the grow lights.

(b) Light is of course essential (unless you are growing mushrooms) - and darkness as well: without a night time to rest, 24/7 lighting will actually bring down your yield. Most vegetables do well with 12-16 hours of light, and the right type and intensity is needed as well. "Leggy" plants usually come from either too little intensity of light or too short a cycle. Sunlight is best, supplemented by artificial light.

Indoor grow lights for the home have traditionally been Fluorescent bulbs, ranging from T12 (1.5" diameter) to T8 (1" diameter). Technological advances have led to T5's (5/8" diameter) - a bulb that is brighter, uses less mercury. Due to the fact that their energy efficiency is measured differently, there is some controversy as to whether they are more energy efficient.

They come in various lengths from six inches to four feet, and need specific T4/T5 fixtures.

The advantage of fluorescent lights are that they are light weight, more efficient than metal halide or sodium lamps, produce less heat and are less expensive. The only downsides are they do contain mercury and must be handled carefully - a broken bulb could contaminate your crop and potting mixture.

More info. On Fluorescent bulbs at http://en.wikipedia.org/wiki/Fluorescent-lamp_formats

LED bulbs are gaining in popularity and lowering in price. Many of these solid state bulbs boast 50,000 hour life spans, far less electricity consumption and overall savings (over the life of the bulb). They can be found in squares, "UFO" circular shapes, 1,2,4 foot "fluorescent tube replacements" - the reason for the quotes is because you have to modify your fixture to run straight AC power from the mains, which means you will need to remove the ballast - a part of the fixture that regulates the current in the fluorescent bulb. Other configurations abound, including direct screw in replacements, floods, spotlights, pars (not to be confused with "PAR") and more.

The advantages of LED bulbs is they typically run cool, last a long time, use less electricity, and are not subject to damage from vibration. They can also be "tuned" to the wavelengths that most plants take advantage of. The main components of light that plants need are in the red spectrum (600-700 nanometers (nm) and blue (400 - 500 nm). While it is popular to create grow lights with only these wavelengths, light from the other wavelengths are also beneficial, including the green spectrum

(500-600nm): *"This investigation demonstrated that the addition of 24% green light (500-600nm) to Red and Blue LEDs (RGB Treatment) enhanced the lettuce growth compared to the plants grown under cool-white fluorescent lamps (CWF treatment). Coincidentally, lettuce grown using RGB lighting would have an additional aesthetic appeal of a green appearance."* Elsewhere in the article they mention that the green spectrum tends to reach the lower parts of the canopy. Through careful measurement, they are able to show that some of this wavelength IS absorbed by the plant instead of being reflected as previously thought.. This wavelength (500-600nm) may help plants that are losing their lowest leaves. (see NASA - http://hortsci.ashspublications.org/content/39/7/1617.full.pdf)

How Close to Place Your Lights:

Light intensity follows the "inverse square law": light intensity decreases exponentially the further away you are from the source. So if you are getting 1000 PAR (Photosynthetically Active Radiation) at 4" from your plant, moving the light 8" away, the plant will only receive 250 PAR. The other consideration is heat: sodium lamps, metal halide lamps and incandescent lamps output a lot of heat - having them too close will burn your plants!

If you are using incandescent grow lights, you want to keep them at least 12" above the plant due to the heat. Fluorescent lights can be as close as 4", and most LED bulbs can be as close as 2". Read your documentation to be sure you are not going to hurt your plants by placing the lights too close.

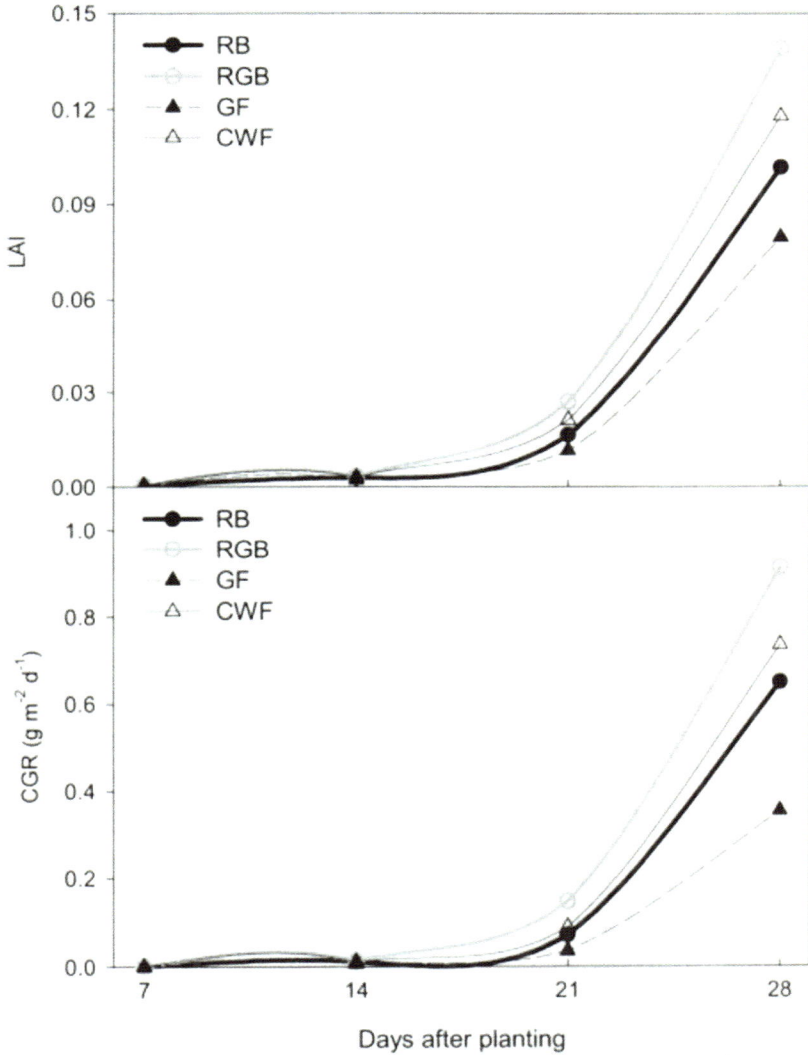

Fig. 2. Leaf area index (LAI) and crop growth rate (CGR) of lettuce grown under red and blue LEDs (RB), red and blue LEDs with green fluorescent lamps (RGB), green fluorescent lamps (GF), and cool-white fluorescent lamps (CWF). The data points are averages of 12 measurements. See Fig. 1 and Table 1 for spectral characteristics.

Further Reading:

- http://www.greenhouse.cornell.edu/crops/factshe ets/SuppLight.pdf
- http://www.egc.com/useful_info_lighting.php

(c) The amount of **heat** your plants need will depend upon the plants themselves. Lettuce and radishes are cool weather plants, tending to bolt if the temperature gets too high. Cucumbers and tomatoes on the other hand, enjoy the warmth and will grow slowly if either the potting mix temperature or the ambient temperature is too low.

Heating the whole house to 80 degrees F is out of the question, so creating an area that has the proper temperature for your plants is the only other option. Many people grow plants in temperature controlled cabinets, adding ventilation and temperature controls as needed.

The soil temperature will affect the germination and growth of your salad garden too. Lettuce like cool soil (60 - 70 degrees F) while tomatoes, cucumbers and melons like warmer soil (up to 80 degrees F). For these plants, you may want to purchase a "heat mat": a heat mat is a flat waterproof electrical appliance that sits under your plant and provides a set amount of warmth for your plants. (see Amazon for many options available – search for "Heat Mat" in Lawn and garden). Soil temperatures can easily be checked using a meat thermometer stuck into the soil.

For those of us less ambitious, there are cool weather varieties of many vegetables, such as "early girl" and "early boy" tomato varieties, and "patio" or "container" varieties. Putting the plant into a "tent" made of plastic or an insulative material also works as long as you make sure there is no chance the light or any supplemental heating source could start a fire. When using a plant tent, you will also need to be sure that there is adequate ventilation so the plants don't get too much humidity and become susceptible to blights and other diseases. Plants also like fresh air, especially the CO_2 rich air we exhale.

There are a number of different tents and cabinets available online from small to room size and prices to fit almost any budget:

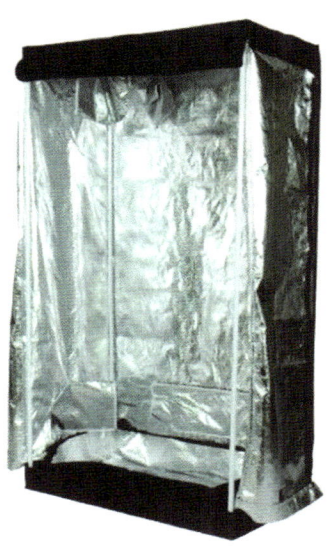

Example of a "grow cabinet" made for use with LED grow lights.

More information:

http://www.cornellcea.com/Horticultural%20information/light.html

(d) Humidity, as mentioned above - can be a problem even in the winter climates. More often than not, there will be too little humidity, drying out the potting mix leading to more frequent watering. Experimentation and the knowledge of your plants needs will be key to maintaining the proper humidity.

(e) Water - If you live in an area that has water piped in, there is probably chlorine and possibly fluorine in your water supply to remove any unwanted pathogens and strengthen your teeth. This is detrimental to your plants but there is a workaround: By drawing the water and letting it sit in an open jug or container, most if not all of the chlorine will dissipate into the air. After a day or two the water will be safe for your plants. Watering will be more frequent indoors, since the indoor humidity in winter will be lower. Be prepared to check your plants every couple of days to make sure you are not stressing your plants with a self made drought.

(f) Growth Medium

Soil mixtures - use a potting MIX, not potting SOIL. The difference is that potting mix has a finer mix of soil and peat moss and contains either perlite or vermiculite or both. Already bought the potting soil? You can add perlite and/or vermiculite to what you have: 2/3 potting soil, 1/3 perlite or 1/3 vermiculite. Screen the soil with 1/4" screen to remove larger pieces if you want to get as close to the store-bought variety as you can.

Soil from your garden should NOT be used without solarizing it and must be mixed with peat moss, vermiculite or perlite unless you have very sandy soil. Here's why: the soil from your garden is host to many creatures and parasites. Bringing in soil from your garden, especially during the fall without having solarized it in the hot summer sun brings all of those creatures in with it. Beetles and other bugs, including cutworms will happily emerge with the warmer indoor weather, mistaking it for spring - flying around your house, eating your sprouts and reproducing without fear of most of the prey that is still dormant outside. Solarizing is simply "cooking" your soil for several weeks before you bring it in. You can take the soil you want to use and put it into black plastic bags, letting the sun bring its temperature up high enough to kill most of the creatures as well as weed seeds and whatever other pathogens may be present in the soil. The downside is that many beneficial organisms suffer the same fate.

Perlite or vermiculite is needed to retain the moisture as well as lessen the compaction of the soil in your containers. Most soils have a large amount of silt and clay: fine particles that clump together and will pull away from the sides of your containers if the soil becomes too dry. The peat moss will help retain the moisture as will the perlite or vermiculite and will "break up" the clumps of clay and silt as long as it's mixed thoroughly, creating air pockets in the soil so the roots can breathe and water can escape.

(g) Containers

You can grow your indoor salad garden in just about any container that will hold your growing medium. You can use milk jugs, soda bottles, baskets lined with plastic , plastic pots (many can be collected at your transfer/recycling station or even at your local garden center in the spring), and good old fashioned clay pots. No matter what you use, you must have drainage holes either in the sides 1-2" above the bottom, or a hole in the bottom of the container that will not become clogged.

Another option is purchasing "self-watering planters". These containers have deeper trays in the bottom and often deeper "legs" that stand in the water that allows the wicking of the water up into the potting mix. They look great, have a special place to add water in the bottom and don't need to be refilled often.

*Search Amazon.com for "*self-watering planter*"*

Photo Credit: climbingcrystal -

http://www.flickr.com/photos/46053374@N05/4515926075/

Used under the Creative Commons Attribution license as of 2013-02-16

The containers will need to have enough depth to hold your growing medium, and will need drainage. Plants need water as well as air in the potting mix - vegetables with their roots standing in in water will get sick and die. Also, do not use any containers that previously held toxic materials (such as used paint cans, varnishes or other volatile chemicals to name a few).

Ideally, a container that is eight to twelve inches deep at a minimum and holding ⅔ cubic feet of potting mix works the best for indoor vegetables. For shallow rooting plants such as lettuces, you can use the pots nurseries use and save more space. These are typically 5" in diameter and 5" deep. A six inch diameter or six by six pot will give you ¾ of a gallon of potting mix -

Available from Amazon.com
Search for "6x6 square white pot" in lawn and garden
Also check: http://www.chulaorchids.com/html/black_pots.html

For those who enjoy square foot gardening, a 12"H x 12"L x 12"W would be the ideal for just about anything you will want to grow. Water will wick up to one foot in most soils. If you have holes in the bottom of your containers, placing a tray or shallow dish underneath the container and placing gravel will aid in humidifying the immediate area too.

Other possibilities include hydroponics and aquaponics, where you grow your plants in an inert material, feeding them their nutrients by either a "drain/fill" method which gives the roots a set amount of time with the water nutrient mixture followed by a set amount of time in the air, a "bubbler system" where you put an air stone in the mixture of nutrients and water allowing the bubbles to pop at the surface of the water essentially "misting" the roots, or a combination of the two using your aquarium's water and the fish's waste to feed the plants. Having little current experience on these options we are not going to delve into this fascinating subject.

(h) **Fertilizer**

Your plants will need nutrients in order to grow as well. Chemical based fertilizers tend to leave salt residue in the potting mix when using containers. A better choice would be an organic liquid fertilizer like liquified kelp or fish emulsion. If you are using prepackaged garden potting mix or potting mix with timed release fertilizer pre-mixed you will probably not need to add any additional fertilizer for up to three months or more, since the water will not be washing away the fertilizer past the tray in the bottom of the container. Read and follow the guidelines on the plant species as well as the fertilizer packaging. For prepared fertilizers, many people use them at ½ strength since many are recommended for outdoor gardens where leaching will occur from rain and irrigation. Experiment with amounts, but don't go over the recommended amounts or frequency of application.

You may also use earthworm castings, ground eggshells, rinsed coffee grounds, etc. either mixed into the potting mix or "side dressing" - which is placing the fertilizer next to (never touching) the plants. Never use meat scraps or oils, as these will only turn rancid and can cause diseases to flourish. Also never use pet waste from dogs or cats. One exception is used aquarium water: when I was keeping a 60 gallon long tank with a nice variety of fish, my plants never looked better!

4. WHEN AND HOW TO GROW AN INDOOR SALAD GARDEN

When Can You Grow an Indoor Salad Garden?

You can grow a salad garden any time of the year! While an outdoor garden is ideal, indoor gardens can give you the advantage of cooler conditions in the summer, and of course warmer conditions in the winter. Planting indoors every two weeks and putting the plants out when the weather is right for them can keep your fingers in the dirt every day of the year.

As we mentioned, another advantage of an indoor garden is shelter - from high winds to wildlife it seems nature is out to get your vegetables before you do! A patio garden is the best of both worlds if you plan it right: make sure you can lift or roll the plants indoors when the need arises.

How Much Room & How Many Salads

How much room you will need to grow a salad per night? This will depend on what you like in your salad. If you just like a "garden salad" with loose leaf lettuces and perhaps some chives for some "zing", you can plant sixteen lettuce plants (four per square foot) and interplant chives between them for four square feet.

To get an even better yield, plant eight lettuce plants per square foot, then when they begin to grow, cut some of the lettuce plants completely once they have six to eight leaves, and once the strongest plants reach eight to ten leaves, pick just the leaves from the strongest plants until there are three or four leaves on the "keepers". You can wash and bag the leaves which will stay fresh in the refrigerator for several days.

Add a tomato plant in another foot square container and two cucumber plants in yet another foot square container for eight square feet of garden in a two by four square foot area. We're borrowing from the "Square Foot Garden" technique here which works well indoors as well as out. If you are making "grow boxes" (see below), three of the 12"x20"x18" deep storage containers side by side would be approximately the amount of space you would need for the larger of these examples. Another variation on this would be to plant a bush type tomato plant in the middle of one of these storage containers and a cucumber plant on either side to save some space, as long as they have something to grow on and don't shade each other out.

5. CREATING A "GROW BOX"

Creating a "grow box" using a storage container is easy, but they become very heavy very fast, especially after you have filled them with water.

The standard method is to create a "reservoir" space in the bottom by cutting the top so it fits about ⅓ of the way up from the bottom. This barrier will separate the soil from the water. A hole cut into the center will be used for the container that will be the "wicking element".

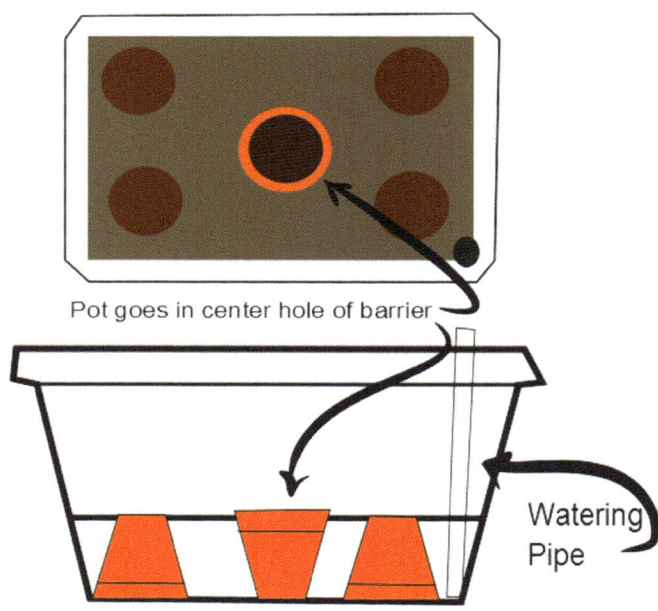

Create a stand that will hold this piece up from the bottom creating a space for the water and still be structurally strong enough to hold up the soil when it's wet. Some people have sacrificed another container by cutting it in half and inverting it, while others just inverted clay pots as columns, putting a piece of rigid plastic down on top. Use your imagination and various recyclable containers or other objects.

Add a wicking element - this is a place where the water and the soil will meet but not mix - you can use a standard plastic pot, a plastic colander, or a piece of drain pipe with holes in the side small enough to let water through but not the potting mix. place this in the center of the barrier.

Make a ¼" hole just below the barrier on the outside of the grow box and either add a hose to drain off the excess (especially if this going to be placed above an electrical element such as a light), or use another lid or tray below it to catch any extra water.

You can also place a pipe through the barrier in one corner making it easy to fill the reservoir.

Fill with your potting mix, set it in place. Wet down the potting mix thoroughly and let it sit for an hour, then check the water level through the watering pipe. fill with more water until the reservoir is at least ¾ full.

The water will wick up through the center "wicking element" and up into the potting mix up to 12 inches, giving your plants enough moisture without having their roots standing in water. Really, it's just a glorified spill tray like you use with regular pots – just hidden away.

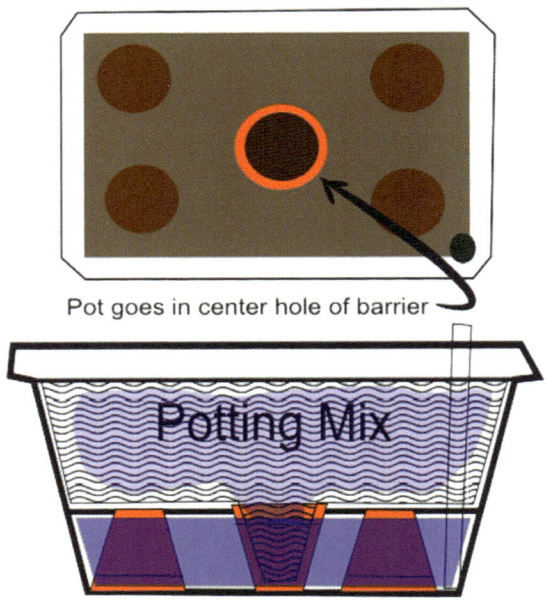

Pot goes in center hole of barrier

When fertilizing, it is best to "side dress" the plants by putting the fertilizer on the top of the soil, not adding it to the water. If you are using a liquid fertilizer, pour the liquid fertilizer around the edges to let it work into the soil. This will not only feed the plants but also any beneficial bacteria in the soil. The roots will naturally grow toward the source of the food, close enough to feed but not so close as to burn themselves (plants are smart that way).

PLANT SPECIFIC NEEDS AND TIPS

6. CUCUMBERS

Cucumbers - 58 - 65 days -- Yield varies, 4 - 5 cucumbers from "Bush Pickle Hybrid", two every two to three weeks from other varieties if they are tended (see notes) for up to 15 per vine plant

Cucumbers fresh from the garden are a treat for just about any salad. With their crunchy fresh taste, They contain Vitamin A, C, and trace elements of niacin and folate, B6, E and K. They also contain the minerals calcium, magnesium, iron, zinc, potassium, phosphorus, copper, manganese, fluoride and more! Their high fiber content along with their water content makes them a healthy addition to any diet.

- **Look for:** Choose a cucumber that is specifically sold to be grown in greenhouses, bush type, and self-pollinating if possible (parthenogenic).
- **Pot Size**: 5 Gallons
- **Plants Per Container: 1**
- **potting mix Amount**: 0.5 cu ft.
- **potting mix Type** - well drained
- **potting mix PH** - Neutral (6)
- **potting mix Temperature** 65 - 85 degrees F (85 degrees is ideal for germination)
- **Air Temperature** 70 degrees F during the day, 60 degrees F at night
- **Fertilizing** fertilize w/ ½ strength liquid fertilizer every two weeks, feed full strength one week after blossoming and again three weeks later **unless** you are using a mix with the fertilizer incorporated into the potting mix..

- **Light Requirements** Full Sun
- **Watering**: water deeply when potting mix on top dries to the touch
- **Notes**: Heavy feeder - If there is a nitrogen deficiency, it will show up as yellowing. If the leaves are brown, this is a sign of a potassium deficiency. Greenhouse cucumbers (vining type) work best when kept pruned to one central leader and trellised . You may have to hand pollinate your cucumbers if they are not parthenogenic. When fruits produce, pinch off extras after two appear. This will give those cucumbers a chance to grow fully. When they are close to maturity, let two more start and cut off the first two.
- **More Information:**
    - http://www.ces.ncsu.edu/hil/hil-8014-b.html
    - www.hort.purdue.edu/ext/ho-8.pdf
    - http://www.actahort.org/books/871/index.htm

7. LETTUCE

Lettuce - 25 - 45 days -- Yield: up to 20 or more leaves per plant or one head

Lettuce, especially romaine and cos varieties are a good source of Riboflavin, Vitamin B6, Calcium, Magnesium, Phosphorus and Copper, and a very good source of Dietary Fiber, Vitamin A, Vitamin C, Vitamin K, Thiamin, Folate, Iron, Potassium and Manganese.

- **Look for**: greenhouse lettuce varieties, bib lettuce, leaf lettuce. Romaine type lettuces include romulus, Signal, Medalion
- **Pot Size:** ½ gallon minimum
- **Plants Per Container:** 1 - you can plant up to five, but you will need to thin them out to one as they grow.
- **potting mix Amount:** .025 cu. ft.
- **potting mix Type**: high organic matter with good water-

holding capacity (extra peat moss/coconut coir plus good compost)

- **potting mix PH:** 6.0 - 6.7
- **potting mix Temperature:** 35 degrees F minimum, 60 - 65 degrees F optimum. At over 80 degrees the germination rate can drop by 50%!
- **Air Temperature**: 60 - 65 degrees F (16 - 18 degrees C)
- **Fertilizing**: when 4-6" tall, use ½ strength if it is not incorporated in the potting mix every two weeks
- **Light Requirements** partial sun
- **Watering**: water regularly and evenly, moist but not soaking soil
- **Notes:** shallow rooting, lettuces can grow in shorter containers. Lettuce likes regular watering and will stress if they are left to dry out. If you are going to be away for awhile, you may wish to add a shallow bowl below the pot filled with gravel and add water liberally
- **Further reading**:
    - http://www.ces.ncsu.edu/hil/hil-11.html
    - http://www.garden.org/ediblelandscaping/?page=2010 11-how-to
    - http://www.hgtv.com/gardening/how-to-plant-an-indoor-salad-garden/index.html
    - http://www.dailypaul.com/262622/how-to-grow-your-own-indoor-winter-salad-garden

8. TOMATOES

Tomato Trade-offs

Tomatoes come in two general varieties: determinate, and indeterminate. In order to have the best salad experience, let's look at the benefits and the drawbacks.

Photo Credit: burgundavia
http://www.flickr.com/photos/coreyburger/4640025475/
Used under the Creative Commons Attributions and Share Alike license as of 2013-02-16

Determinate varieties

- tend to ripen their fruits all at once (within a two week

period), then die.
- are a "bush" variety, tending to grow only to about four feet maximum
- may only require a minimum amount of caging if at all
- should not be pruned as this reduces the crop, but it also reduces the maintenance.

Indeterminate varieties

- are "vining" varieties
- will produce fruits until frost
- can reach 10 feet or more (see "<u>How to Grow World Record Tomatoes: A Guinness Champion Reveals His All-Organic Secrets</u>")
- need caging/training
- must be pruned of "suckers" to increase yield (and decrease the chance of it taking over your house!)

For determinate tomato varieties, plant every two weeks for a more or less constant supply. This of course can take up a lot of room, but if you like a lot of tomatoes, it's the way to go!

For indeterminates, plant them as soon as you can, and keep them trimmed of suckers. One great trick if you have the room is to train the indeterminate tomato plant up a piece of thick twine connected to the ceiling. Be sure to loop the twine up and over the eye hook, then back down again, because as the plant grows, you will be lowering the string, keeping the tomato plant in the most sun or light, and letting the stem reach the potting mix surface - the stem will take root.

Tomato Sizes

Full size "beef steak" tomatoes can make you the envy of all of your neighbors, but it may be spring before you get any. Cherry, "pear", and plum size will fruit more quickly and give you more tomatoes over a longer period of time, especially the indeterminate variety. Recommend planting both the smaller cherry tomatoes for the immediate enjoyment and some of the extra-early varieties to enjoy later.

Nutritionally, tomatoes are a good source of vitamin E, B6, A, C, K, Thiamine, Niacin, Folate, Magnesium, Phosphorus and Copper.

Tomatoes - 60 - 90 days -- Yield varies greatly depending on variety

- **Look for**: determinate or indeterminate, greenhouse friendly, early girl, better boy, and other short season types for full size tomatoes, just about any pear or cherry tomato varieties.
- **Pot Size**: 5 gallon minimum
- **Plants Per Container**: 1
- **potting mix**: 0.5 cu. ft.
- **potting mix Type**: well drained, friable (crumbles easily), rich in compost
- **potting mix PH**: between 5.5 & 6.8
- **potting mix Temperature:** Minimum of 60 degrees F, Optimum 80 degrees F
- **Air Temperature**: between 70 degrees F and 85 degrees F
- **Fertilizing:** if you are planting a seedling from the store, put a small amount of tomato fertilizer in the planting hole (1/2 handful). If you're starting from seed, start them in peat pots and then follow the above directions. If you find

you are getting yellowing leaves at the bottom of the plant, it's time to add more fertilizer. Do this about 3 - 4" away from the plant in a circle. Apply more fertilizer once the fruit has formed,   Continue to fertilize at ½ strength every 3 - 4 weeks until the plant is done producing (determinate), or you find sharing your home with a tomato plant a bit like the little shop of horrors, and transplant it outside.

- **Light Requirements**: Full Sun
- **Watering**: Water deeply (thoroughly) but infrequently. Let the top of the soil dry out on the surface.
- Notes: Wash hands before you touch your plant if you smoke, Do not use tomato cages from outdoors if previous year's tomatoes had any blight. If they did, use a blow torch and heat every inch of the cage, going over every inch. This is the only way we know of to kill the blight.

9. CHIVES AND ONIONS

Chives/Onions - 40 - 80 days -- Varies - cut and come will extend growing season

Chives are the smallest cousins of onions. Used mainly for the greens, chives add a great flavor to salads and other foods. Chives are a good source of Thiamin, Niacin, Pantothenic Acid, Phosphorus and Zinc, as well as other minerals.

- **Look for:** bunching onions, leeks, chives, garlic chives
- **Pot Size:** ½ gallon minimum
- **Plants Per Container:** 6 - 10
- **potting mix:** 0.05 cu. ft
- **potting mix Type:** likes fast draining soil - add more perlite
- **potting mix PH:** 6.0 - 8.0
- **potting mix Temperature:** 50 degrees F minimum, 75 degrees F optimum
- **Air Temperature:** 60 - 70 degrees F
- **Fertilizing:** ½ strength or less - twice per month. Any more will lessen the flavor
- **Light Requirements:** partial to full sun
- **Watering:** keep moist but not soaking wet. The potting mix should be able to clump but not have so much water that you can wring it out
- **Notes:** likes the company of other plants, especially indoors - this aids in keeping the humidity up. Helps if they sit in pebble trays. Misting helps when humidity is real low. Acts as a repellent for most bugs, but a spray of soapy water will deter any persistent bugs.

- ○ **TIP**: buy chives or small bunching onions in the store, cut ½" from the root and plant the roots down, with the top that was cut just showing. Keep watered, and the chives will restart. Pick up pearl onions when they are on sale and plant the bulbs whole with just the pointy top showing above the soil. In a few weeks they will be growing well!

- More Information:
    - ○ http://ucanr.edu/sites/MarinMG/?story=888

10. BROCCOLI RABE

Broccoli Rabe (raab) (pronounced "Rob") 40 - 50 days -- Yield - one to two plants per serving

Broccoli Raab are part of the brassica family (the same family as broccoli, but a different species). Highly nutritious and full of phytochemicals, vitamin C and beta-carotene. Mostly used for stir frys and sautéed, when picked young enough and used sparingly it can make a great addition to salads.

- **Look for:** "Spring Raab", Spigariello Liscia, Sessantina Grossa, Broccoli Rapini, Brocoletti
- **Pot Size:** 1 gallon minimum, better in 2 - 5 gallon size
- **Plants Per Container:** 1
- **potting mix:** 0.1 cu. ft.
- **potting mix Type:** fertile well drained soil (add compost, worm castings if available - heavy feeder)
- **potting mix PH**: 6.5 - 7.5
- **potting mix Temperature:** prefers 45-65
- **Air Temperature:** 50 - 85 degrees F
- **Fertilizing**: Every two weeks, add extra nitrogen or use a 10-5-5 type fertilizer
- **Light Requirements:** partial to full sun - some people note that if the temperature is above 85 degrees F and you have full sun, they will stop producing leaves and begin to bolt
- **Watering:** regular watering, can wait until the top ¾" of soil is dry
- **Notes:** Pick whole plant when buds appear, or pick just the buds for an extended harvest. Greens used in salad mix.

11. CARROTS

Carrots - 70 - 75 days -- Yield - up to 12 per five gallon container

Carrots are one of the most popular root crops in the garden. They come in several lengths and colors, including white, yellow, red, purple and several shades of orange. Rich in vitamin A, the red variety like "Red Rocket" can contain ten to fifteen times more beta carotene than the yellow varieties.

- **Look for:** short to medium varieties, "nectar", "Bolero", "Caracas", "Touchon"
- **Pot Size**: 5 gallon
- **Plants Per Container:** up to 12
- **potting mix:** 0.5 cu. ft.
- **potting mix Type:** mix in 1 part sand to 3 parts potting mix
- **potting mix PH:** 6.0 - 6.8
- **potting mix Temperature:** minimum 50 degrees F, Optimal 75 degrees F
- **Air Temperature:** 60 - 85 degrees F
- **Fertilizing**: feed once per month to once every 6 weeks
- **Light Requirements**: full sun
- **Watering:** must be kept moist - a 1 - 2" layer of mulch over the top will help especially indoors
- **Notes:** mix 1 part radish seeds to 1 part carrot seeds - radishes will be ready before the carrots, and the carrots will appreciate the extra room when their neighbors are invited to dinner!
- Further Reading:
  - http://www.carrotmuseum.co.uk/cultivation2.html

12. MICRO GREENS

Micro Greens - 7 - 14 days -- Yield - one to two servings per pint, more if used sparingly with other greens.

Micro greens are a mixture of different plants picked when the plant is immature to provide flavor and nutrients as well as texture and visual appeal to your salads.

Extremely easy to grow, salad greens include mustard greens, beet greens, arugula, minutina, miniature Chinese cabbages, watercress, tatsoi, and what until recently have been thought of as weeds like purselane, miner's lettuce dandelion, claytonia, and others.

Growing microgreens is the quickest and easiest garden

experience you will have, and it's great for kids, too! You can grow them in a small salad container, they take only 7 to 14 days to grow, since you harvest them right after their first true leaves appear.

- **Look for**: micro-greens, microgreens
- **Pot Size**: pint, preferably repurposed fruit containers
- **Plants Per Container**: many
- **potting mix**: ½ potting mix, ½ seedling mix
- **potting mix** Type: see above
- **potting mix PH:** 6.0 - 7.0
- **potting mix Temperature:** 35 degrees minimum, room temperature is optimal
- **Air Temperature:** 60 - 80 degrees F
- **Fertilizing:** no need
- **Light Requirements:** after sprouting, partial to full sun
- **Watering:** bottom water by setting the container in ½ depth of water for one minute. Takes daily watering. Also keep a spray bottle handy to mist the tops.
- **Notes:** since these are seedlings, they are very susceptible to drying out. A soft terrycloth towel over the top or paper towel soaked in water and wrung out. Cut close to the top of the soil. Use immediately after carefully and thoroughly washing.
- **Further Reading:**
   - http://www.newsdesk.umd.edu/scitech/release.cfm?ArticleID=2771
   - http://agnr.umd.edu/news/mighty-microgreens
   - http://www.markbraunstein.org/growmicrogreens.htm
   - http://greenharvest.com.au/SproutingAndMicrogreens/MicrogreensGrowingInformation.html

13. VEGETABLE GREENS

Vegetable Greens - 30 - 60 days -- Yield: varies

Vegetable greens are the big brothers of the micro greens. Taking a bit longer to grow, these can be picked a few leaves at a time to extend the harvest almost indefinitely. The flavor of the greens are milder, and you can also use many of the greens in stir-fry as well as salads.

- **Look for**: "Green Wave", minutina, summer komatsuna, watercress, tatsoi, purselane, "red giant", arugula, claytonia, surrey, red leaf vegetable amaranth, greens mix, "vit"
- **Pot Size**: ½ gallon to 1 gallon, depending on the size of the plant you want
- **Plants Per Container**: 1 - 2
- **potting mix:** 0.05 to 0.1 cu. ft
- **potting mix Type**: well drained
- **potting mix PH**: varies depending on the green, but 6.0 to 7.0 works well
- **potting mix Temperature**: 60 degrees F minimum
- **Air Temperature**: 60 - 85 degrees F
- **Fertilizing**: for the brassica family, an extra dose of nitrogen will help it along, but follow the directions on the fertilizer and cut by ½. Plants such as arugula, purselane and watercress don't need much as far as fertilizer goes, but if you are finding yellowing leaves you may want to add ½ dose of a balanced fertilizer.
- **Light Requirements**: Partial to full sun

- **Watering**: water gently and mist until the first true leaves appear, keeping them covered with a clear polyethylene sheet or plastic wrap until you see growth.
- **Notes**: You can find mixes of different greens that include mustards, brassicas and various lettuces. You don't need deep containers for these plants - using a shallow storage bin with the proper drainage allows you to plant two square feet of mixed greens easily. Planting three of these containers a week apart allows you to harvest almost continuously, especially if you pick the mature leaves instead of removing the whole plant.

14. BEANS, SNAP

Beans, Snap - 50 - 70 days -- Yield varies by type

Beans are a great source of vitamin A, Folates, B6, B-12, thiamine, vitamin C, also a good source of iron, calcium, magnesium, manganese and potassium. Great steamed, dipped, freshly washed and french cut, as well as right off the vine.

- **Look for:** bush varieties, vining varieties. "Providor" is one of our favorites.
- **Pot Size:** 2 gallons
- **Plants Per Container:** 2
- **potting mix:** rich, 0.2 cu. ft.
- **potting mix Type**: well drained, high organic content
- **potting mix PH:** 6.0 - 7.0
- **potting mix Temperature:** 60 degrees F minimum, 80 degrees F optimum
- **Air Temperature**: 60 degrees F to 85 degrees F
- **Fertilizing**: Every two weeks with ½ recommended dosage
- **Light Requirements**: full sun
- **Watering**: Once the plants are established, water deeply when the potting mix is dry 1 - 2" below the top.
- **Notes**: you will want to plant at least eight plants at a time, otherwise you will only have enough for a light meal every few days. While beans store well in the fridge, if you can manage the space, the more plants the better. While root binding is not usually an issue, competition for light is. If they are too crowded, the yield will be low. Consider interplanting lettuce or other low growing vegetables between them.
- **Further reading**:
  - http://ag.arizona.edu/pubs/garden/mg/vegetable/container.html

15. PEAS

Peas - 60 - 70 days Yield -- varies by plant, but we've gotten up to 12 oz per plant (approximately 25 - 30)

You can find many varieties of peas that work well in containers. "Tom Thumb" is a popular variety, as are "Little Marvel" and "Early Frosty". Our favorite are the snow peas like "Oregon Sugar Pod", "Dwarf Grey Sugar Pea", and our outdoor favorite "Oregon Giant" which can be grown indoors too. Nutritionally peas are an excellent source of folic acid, Vitamin C, beta-sitosterol, vitamin K, vitamin A, and many anti-oxidants and other minerals.

Photo Credit: Essyeyre -
http://www.flickr.com/photos/54912928@N06/5087112309/

Used under the Creative Commons Attribution License as of 2013/02/16

- **Look for:** Bush varieties, low growing vining type

- **Pot Size**: 1 gallon
- **Plants Per Container**: 2
- **potting mix**: 0.1 cu ft
- **potting mix Type**: well drained, rich in organic content
- **potting mix PH**: 6.0 - 7.0
- **potting mix Temperature**: 40 degrees F minimum, 75 degrees F optimum
- **Air Temperature**: 60 degrees F to 75 degrees F
- **Fertilizing**: If not using a time-release fertilizer, find an organic fertilizer with added nutrients like copper, zinc, molybdenum. Fertilize ½ strength every two to three weeks
- **Light Requirements**: partial to full sun
- **Watering**: keep soil moist, water regularly
- **Notes**: You will want to plant six to eight pea plants at each planting, and plant them every two to three weeks. After they have set fruit, the peas will stop producing. Heat will also stop them from producing, as they are a cool weather plant.
- **Further Reading:**
    - http://www.clemson.edu/extension/hgic/plants/vegetables/crops/hgic1328.html
    - http://www.extension.umn.edu/distribution/horticulture/M1249.html

16. PEPPERS

Peppers, Bell 50 - 70 days -- Yield: two peppers per plant, sometimes more; smaller sweet or hot peppers: depends on variety

Bell peppers are part of the **Capsicum** annuum family. The bell peppers are mild and sweet, mostly grown for eating raw in salads as well as grilled, fried, sautéed, mixed in sauces and more. Having an abundance of vitamin C, vitamin A, antioxidants alpha and beta carotenes and more.

- **Look for**: extra early varieties like "Ace" (only 50 days to green, 70 days to red
- **Pot Size**: 2 gallon
- **Plants Per Container**: 1
- **potting mix**: 0.2 cu ft.
- **potting mix Type**: well drained, high organic content
- **potting mix PH:**
- **potting mix Temperature**: Minimum of 70 degrees F
- **Air Temperature**: 70 degrees F to 85 degrees F.
- Fertilizing: fertilize after first full leaves appear, and again when you see the flowers with ½ recommended dose.
- **Light Requirements**: Full Sun
- **Watering:** water frequently, do not let the soil dry out. Don't over water - peppers don't like standing in water.
- **Notes:** You won't often get more than two peppers per plant, and you will have to pollinate them yourself with a q-tip. Likes humidity. Tip: When you first plant, add some crushed/pulverized eggshells around the pepper plant by drying out the eggshells and running them through a

blender until powdered.

17. SPINACH

Spinach - 30 - 45 days -- Yield 1/2 servings baby spinach per ½ gallon container, one to two servings per plant if left to mature.

One of the most satisfying cool weather crops, spinach produces large yields of nutritious dark green leaves that are excellent in salads as well as cooking. Many sandwich shops now carry "baby spinach leaves" - the first or second set of true leaves that appear. Succession planting is the best way to keep yourself supplied, though if you like the larger leaves you can pick the outer leaves once they have reached eight to ten leaves.

Full of Protein, Vitamin A, Vitamin C, Vitamin E (Alpha Tocopherol), Vitamin K. Also contains Thiamin, Riboflavin, Vitamin B6, Folate, Calcium, Iron, Magnesium, Phosphorus, Potassium, Copper and Manganese,

- **Look for**: smooth leaf spinach varieties include "Emu", "Nordic" "Olympia" and "Space". Savoyed (crinkled leaf) include "Indian Summer", "Donkey", "Tyee",
- **Pot Size**: ½ gallon minimum, consider growing in low storage bin type container with good drainage (6" x 12" x 20"), especially if you are planning on "baby spinach"
- **Plants Per Container**: 1 plant every 3", though you can over-plant and harvest the thinnings.
- **potting mix:** 0.05 cu. ft. per ½ gallon container, approximately 1 cu ft per low storage bin.

- **potting mix Type**: well drained - consider adding 1 part perlite or vermiculite to two parts potting mix
- potting mix PH: 6.5 - 7.5
- **potting mix Temperature**: 35 degrees minimum, 68 degrees optimum
- **Air Temperature**: 55 degrees F to 75 degrees F
- **Fertilizing**: Once every two weeks, ½ strength
- **Light Requirements**: 6 - 8 hours full sun
- **Watering**: Needs to be evenly moist throughout growing season.
- **Notes**: Spinach will bolt and grow erratically if the soil gets too warm. If you are growing your spinach in a southern facing window, consider shading the container with a piece of cardboard or other containers.

18. STRAWBERRIES

Photo Credit: Bev Wagar. http://www.flickr.com/photos/greengardenvienna/5276114316/
Used under the Creative Commons Attribution license as of 2013/02/16

Many strawberries begin fruiting the second year after planting, but they can be fun to grow indoors, especially if you have a strawberry bed outside that sends out runners. Getting starts from a garden center or on line instead of starting from seeds will give you a "shortcut" to delicious strawberries you can't pick more locally! Strawberries can be a fun winter growing project, especially if you have kids. The only issue will be having any left over for yourself! Getting enough strawberry plants growing at the same time can be difficult. Many people use hanging planters, while others "grow vertically" - using PVC pipes and grow their strawberries up a tower or two. Still others have drilled holes in the sides of five gallon buckets and fit up to 25 plants in one bucket! (see "further reading" below for link). Eight strawberries have more vitamin C than an orange. Also a good source of manganese, and potassium.

- Look for: Day Neutral varieties if you want strawberries all season long. Also there are Alpine varieties that do not send out runners, have tiny flavor packed strawberries and are "everbearing" - this is different than day-neutral, as they set fruit twice instead of all season long.
- Pot Size: ½ gallon minimum - larger containers will work better since strawberry plants can share the root space
- Plants Per Container: 2
- potting mix: .025 cu ft.
- potting mix Type: well drained, high organic content
- potting mix PH: 5.5 - 6.5, 6.0 being optimal.
- potting mix Temperature: 60 degrees F to 80 degrees F
- Air Temperature: 60 degrees F to 80 degrees F
- Fertilizing: a weak solution (¼ to ½ strength when flowering and bearing fruit)
- Light Requirements: full sun, 12 - 16 hours per day
- Watering: Keep soil moist but not soggy
- Notes: Aphids & spider mites will often be the pest sources of indoor strawberries. An insecticidal soap usually takes care of these. Follow the package directions. For transplants, be sure you pinch off any flowers for the first six weeks - this forces the plant to concentrate on creating roots & will give you healthier plants overall. Planting more in larger containers allows for sharing of water resources as well as packing more plants in the same area.
- Further reading http://mckarion.wordpress.com/2010/01/30/frugal-garden-strawberry-bucket/

19. SWISS CHARD

Swiss Chard - 28 baby - 55 bunching -- Yield: ½ serving per ½ gallon container baby, one serving per plant if left to grow.

Swiss chard is more popular than spinach! With a similar flavor but a multitude of colors to it's thick crunchy stalk and broad green leaves, they are a feast for the eyes as well as the palate. One concern with Swiss chard is that it contains measureable amounts of "oxalates". Persons with existing and untreated kidney or gallbladder problems may want to avoid eating Swiss chard, as the oxalates in high enough quantities can crystalize, causing health problems. On the nutrition side, Swiss chard is a good source of thiamine, folate, phosphorus and zinc, as well as a very good source of dietary fiber. Also vitamin A, C, E, K, B6 and a number of minerals.

- **Look for**: "Bright Lights", "Ruby Red", "Bright Yellow", "Magenta Sunset"
- **Pot Size**: ½ gallon minimum
- **Plants Per Container**: plant 4 - 6" between seeds
- **potting mix**: 0.025 cu. ft.
- **potting mix Type**: well drained, high organic content
- **potting mix PH**: 6.0 - 6.8
- **potting mix Temperature**: 50 degrees F minimum, 85 degrees optimal
- **Air Temperature**:60 degrees F to 85 degrees F
- **Fertilizing:** fertilize every two weeks ½ strength
- **Light Requirements**: Full sun
- **Watering**: likes moist soil, water regularly

- **Notes**: Leaves are most tender when young. Can be shredded finely for salad. Like carrots, Swiss chard is biennial - it will grow vegetatively the first year, then set seed in the second.
- **Further reading:**
  - http://www.whfoods.com/genpage.php?tname=foodspice&dbid=16
  - http://urbanext.illinois.edu/veggies/chard.cfm

20. HERBS

Pound for pound, herbs are some of the most expensive plant products you can buy. Take a look at the cost per pound, and you will be growing most of your own herbs in a heart-beat! After the shock wears off, you will realize that you don't eat pounds of herbs, and your visions of living in a spice and herb greenhouse mansion will resize itself to a reasonable size of several pots. Basil, oregano, sage, parsley and cilantro are the most popular leafy herbs for cooking as well as salad dressings.

Photo Credit: Hair Squared
http://www.flickr.com/photos/hair_squared/3804321959/
Used under Creative Commons Attribution and Share Alike License as of 2013/0215

- **Look for**: Herbs you use in your cooking most often
- **Pot Size**: 1 quart minimum
- **Plants Per Container**: space seeds about 1" apart, thin as the plants mature
- **potting mix**: 0.0125 cu. ft.
- **potting mix Type:** well drained
- **potting mix PH**: 6.0 - 7.0
- **potting mix Temperature**: 45 degrees F - 70 degrees F
- **Air Temperature**: 45 degrees F - 70 degrees F
- **Fertilizing**: minimal
- **Light Requirements:** partial to full sun, at least 4-5 hours
- **Watering:** After the plants have their first full leaves, let the soil dry to about ½" before watering to promote good root growth. Overwatering and over-fertilizing can be detrimental to most herbs.
- **Notes**: Many herbs can be grown continuously, cutting sprigs or leaves as needed. Pinching off the tops of many herbs will promote side growth creating bushier plants. Herbs are about the most forgiving plants you can grow indoors

21. COMMON INDOOR PLANT AILMENTS AND CURES

Indoor plants are not immune to disease or the environment despite how much coddling they receive. Here are a few common problems you may encounter with indoor vegetables.

Too much water!

Here is an example of too much water or poor drainage with a basil plant. If a plant's roots sit in the soil it will drown! The roots will begin to rot and it will not be able to bring the nutrients it needs to the rest of the plant.

Too Little Water

Too little water will often result in the plants leaves starting at the edges turning brown, sparse new growth.

BUGS!

You may find bugs on the plants or in the soil. Look under the leaves too, they may not want to show themselves.

Photo Credit: Waldo Jaquith
http://www.flickr.com/photos/waldoj/172095176/
Used under the Creative Commons Attribution and Share Alike License as of 2013/02/15

- You could dust your plants with diatomaceous earth, but

don't breathe it in as it is a lung irritant.

- Insecticidal soaps (potassium fatty acid soaps) work if sprayed directly on the soft bodied insect. NOTE: Mustard/brassicae/cabbage are very sensitive to soaps, avoid using on these plants.
- Fruit flies can be controlled by removing any rotting vegetation and making an insect trap

Photo Credit: Wikimedia Commons

- Sawdust works as a deterrent against onion flies, carrot flies and cabbage flies
- Carrot disks work against click beetles and crane flies
- Find the specific bug that has invaded and research the best non-toxic remedies.
-

Further Reading:

- http://www.garden.org/pestlibrary/
- http://vegipm.tamu.edu/imageindex.html

- http://www.ipm.ucdavis.edu/PMG/menu.homegarden.html

Diseases

Diseased plants should be removed immediately and their source found if possible. Tomatoes can suffer especially from both early and late blight if you have brought infected soil or cages in from outdoors. Powdery mildew can affect squash onions, gourds, strawberries and melons. Lessening the humidity will help control the spread, but removal of the plant and it's potting mix is the best cure. Planting powdery mildew resistant varieties is also recommended.

Too Little Light/Not Long Enough Cycle

Too little light or not a long enough light cycle will result in "leggy" seedlings and plants. Sometimes the remedy is as simple as moving the light closer to the plant, but if the plants are too close to the light the leaves will dry out or worse - become a fire hazard!

Not Enough Nutrients/Too Much Fertilizer or Amendments

Just like an outdoor garden, if your plants don't receive enough nutrients they will be stunted or just wither and die. If your plants have too much, their roots can "burn" - this is a chemical burn, not combustion. Getting a pH and NPK (Nitrogen, Potassium, and Phosphorus) test kit can save you a lot of heartache. Test the soil as stated in the directions on your test kit before you plant, and take a sample from the edge of your container just as the plants are flowering if you are growing a fruiting variety to find out if there are any of the vital nutrients that are lacking in your potting mix, then add sparingly - since these are indoor plants, the nutrients don't wash away as quickly.

Nutritional Reference Sites:

http://nutritiondata.self.com/

http://health.learninginfo.org/nutrition-facts/index.htm

http://www.nutrientfacts.com/

ABOUT THE AUTHOR

Andrew Perkins is an avid gardener in Western Massachusetts. A parent, scrimshander (scrimshaw artist) and computer support specialist, Andrew shares his garden with family, friends and a bear that enjoys sitting in the middle of his corn patch for a midnight snack.

Made in the USA
Lexington, KY
14 November 2013